United States Presidents

Election 2000: A Lesson in Civics

Bob Italia

ABDO Publishing Company

visit us at
www.abdopub.com

Published by ABDO Publishing Company, 4940 Viking Drive, Edina, Minnesota 55435.

Printed in the United States.

Photo Credits: AP/Wide World, Corbis, TimePix

Contributing Editors: Tamara L. Britton, Kate A. Furlong, Christine Fournier
Art Direction: Neil Klinepier

Library of Congress Cataloging-in-Publication Data

Italia, Bob, 1955-
Election 2000 : a lesson in civics / Bob Italia.
p. cm. -- (The United States presidents)
Includes index.
ISBN 1-57765-576-1
1. Presidents--United States--Election--2000--Juvenile literature. [1. Presidents--Election--2000. 2. Politics, Practical.] I. Title. II. United States presidents (Edina, Minn.)

JK526 2000c
324.973'0929--dc21

2001016121

Contents

Part I

Election 2000: A Historic Event 4
The Candidates 6
Election Day 8
The Recounts 10
The Florida Supreme Court 12
Racing the Clock 14
The U.S. Supreme Court 16
Decision 18
Election 2000 Timeline 20

Part II

A Lesson in Civics 22
Glossary 47
For Further Reading 47
Internet Sites 48
Index 48

A NOTE TO THE READER:

Some words in this book are highlighted.

- The **RED** words are explained in Part II (see page 23).
- The **BLUE** words are explained in the Glossary (see page 47).

Part I

Election 2000: A Historic Event

Election 2000 was a historic battle for the **presidency**. Only one other election has been so bitterly contested. It was the 1876 election between **Republican** Rutherford B. Hayes and **Democrat** Samuel Tilden.

Tilden won the **popular vote**. But the votes from Florida, Louisiana, and South Carolina were contested. Both Democrats and Republicans accused each other of cheating.

For weeks, the **U.S. Congress debated** the election. The year ended. Congress could not decide what to do.

Then Congress appointed an **electoral commission**. It would choose the winner of the contested electoral votes. Eight Republicans and seven Democrats served on the commission. They voted eight to seven to give the votes to Hayes.

On March 2, 1877, the commission announced the results. Hayes had 185 electoral votes. Tilden had 184. Two days later, Hayes took the oath of office.

In 2000, Republican George W. Bush and Democrat Al Gore also had a close election. Just like in 1876, Florida's votes were in question. And each **candidate** needed the state's electoral votes to win.

But in 2000, Congress did not appoint an electoral commission. Instead, for the first time in history, the **U.S. Supreme Court** helped decide the winner.

RED - page 23 BLUE - page 47

STEPHEN
BREYER

SANDRA DAY
O'CONNOR

RUTH BADER
GINSBURG

ANTHONY
KENNEDY

WILLIAM
REHNQUIST

ANTONIN
SCALIA

DAVID
SOUTER

JOHN PAUL
STEVENS

CLARENCE
THOMAS

The nine U.S. Supreme Court justices who made election history

ELECTION 200

The Candidates

In 2000, many **candidates** ran for **president**. But only two were on the **ballot** in every state. They were **Republican** George W. Bush and **Democrat** Al Gore.

George W. Bush

George Walker Bush was born on July 6, 1946, in New Haven, Connecticut. Bush is the oldest son of past U.S. president George Bush and his wife, Barbara.

Bush studied at Yale University. He graduated in 1968. Then he served as a pilot in the Texas Air National Guard.

Bush earned a business degree from Harvard University in 1975. Two years later, he started an oil company. Then he married Laura Welch.

In 1978, Bush ran for a seat in the U.S. **House of Representatives**. But Bush lost the **election**. So he returned to his oil company. But business was slow. So he sold the company in 1984. Then he worked for another oil company.

In 1988, Bush worked on his father's presidential **campaign**. His father easily won the election. Then Bush returned to Texas. In 1989, he became a co-owner of the Texas Rangers baseball team.

In 1994, Bush ran for governor of Texas. He won the election. Texans liked Bush. They re-elected him in 1998. In 2000, the Republican **party nominated** Bush for president.

RED - page 23 BLUE - page 47

Albert Gore, Jr., was born on March 31, 1948, in Washington, D.C. His parents were Albert and Pauline Gore. His father served in the U.S. **House of Representatives** and **Senate**.

Gore grew up in both Carthage, Tennessee, and Washington, D.C. He graduated from Harvard University in 1969. Then he joined the U.S. Army. In 1970, he married Mary Elizabeth "Tipper" Aitcheson. He served five months in the Vietnam War as an army journalist in 1971.

From 1971 to 1976, Gore wrote for the *Tennessean* newspaper. He reported on local news. During this time, Gore also attended Vanderbilt University.

Al Gore

Gore won a seat in the U.S. House of Representatives in 1976. He was **re-elected** three times. Gore won election to the U.S. Senate in 1984.

In 1988, Gore ran for **president**. But he did not have enough support to continue his **campaign**. So he served in the U.S. Senate until 1992. That year, he wrote a book called *Earth in the Balance*.

Then from 1992 to 2000, Gore served as vice president under President Bill Clinton. In June 1999, Gore announced he would again run for president. He won the **Democratic nomination** for the 2000 election.

Election Day

On November 7, 2000, Americans went to their local **polling places**. They cast their **ballots** for **president**. Before the polling places closed, television stations projected each state's winner. They did this by conducting **exit polls**.

First, the stations projected that Gore had won Florida's 25 **electoral votes**. Later, they took back that announcement. Then they said the state was too close to call.

After all the polling places closed, Bush had won more states than Gore. But most of Gore's states had many electoral votes. Late that night, Bush had 246 electoral votes. Gore had 260. The winner needed 270. The **candidate** who won Florida's 25 electoral votes would win the **election**.

All of Florida's ballots were finally counted by the early morning of November 8. The stations declared Bush the winner in Florida. Gore called Bush to **concede** defeat.

But the election had been close. Bush had won by fewer than 2,000 votes. In such a close election, Florida law required a machine recount.

Gore thought he still might have a chance to win after all the ballots were recounted. So he called Bush and took back his concession. Florida election officials again ran the ballots through the counting machines. Bush's lead shrank to fewer than 600 votes.

RED - page 23 BLUE - page 47

On election day, citizens cast their votes for president.

The Recounts

Gore was not happy with the machine recount. The counting machines had rejected thousands of **ballots**. Some of the ballots were not marked clearly. The machines could not tell who the **citizen** intended to **vote** for.

So on November 9, Gore asked for a hand recount of ballots in four Florida **counties**. The counties were Volusia, Palm Beach, Broward, and Dade. Gore felt that hand recounts would be more **accurate** than the machine recounts. And he hoped he might gain enough votes to win.

A Florida election official inspects a ballot.

Bush felt that the machine recount had been fair. He thought a hand recount would break the **law**. So Bush filed a **lawsuit** on November 11. He asked a **U.S. District Court** judge to block any hand recounts.

In court, Bush's **lawyers** said the hand recounts were **unconstitutional**. The Fourteenth **Amendment** says that the law equally protects each citizen. Florida had no rules on recounting ballots by hand. So citizens' votes might not be counted equally in each county. But on November 13, the judge refused to stop the hand recounts. He said **elections** were a **state** issue, not a **federal** issue.

The four counties continued their hand recounts. They had to give new vote totals to Florida's **secretary of state**, Katherine Harris, by November 14. Volusia and Palm Beach Counties did not think they could meet the deadline. So they filed a **lawsuit** with a Florida **circuit court**. They wanted more time to finish their hand recounts.

On November 14, the circuit court refused to extend the deadline. But it also said Harris had to accept hand-recounted **votes** if the **counties** had a good reason for missing the deadline.

Harris said the counties had unacceptable reasons for being late. So she **certified** Florida's **election** results without the hand-recounted **ballots**. Bush had won by 300 votes.

Katherine Harris

Harris planned to certify the official vote total on November 18. It would include the **absentee ballots**. Harris refused to add any late votes from the hand recounts to the official vote total. But some counties continued with their recounts anyway.

Bush asked a state circuit court to stop all hand recounts. The court said no. So on November 16, Bush **appealed** to the **U.S. Circuit Court of Appeals** in Atlanta. He again said the recounts were **unconstitutional** under the Fourteenth **Amendment**.

Gore claimed the recounts were a **state** issue, not a **federal** issue. So he thought the decision should be made in a Florida court. He believed the Tenth Amendment proved this. The U.S. Circuit Court of Appeals agreed with Gore. The recounts continued.

Meanwhile, Gore filed a lawsuit against Harris in a Florida circuit court. He wanted to stop Harris from certifying the state's votes. He thought the court should allow the hand-recounted votes as part of the state's official vote total. But Gore lost the lawsuit. The judge said Harris's decision to not count the votes was legal.

The Florida Supreme Court

By November 17, the **absentee ballots** were ready to be counted. Harris planned to **certify** the state's official **vote** total on November 18. But Gore **appealed** to the Florida **Supreme Court**. It agreed to hold a **hearing** on November 20. Until then, the court stopped Harris from certifying the state's votes.

On November 21, the Florida Supreme Court ruled. It said the recounts could continue. It also said that Harris must include the votes from the recounted **ballots** in the state's official vote total. The court said the four **counties** must complete hand recounts by 5 P.M. on November 26.

Bush disliked the new deadline of November 26. Florida **law** said the vote must be certified on November 18, 2000. Bush thought the new deadline was illegal because courts cannot make new laws. That is the **legislature's** job.

So on November 22, Bush filed a **lawsuit** with the U.S. Supreme Court. He wanted to stop the hand recounts. Two days later, the court agreed to hear Bush's appeal. But the hearing would not take place until the first week of December.

Meanwhile, Florida **election** workers recounted the ballots. They looked at each ballot that the counting machines had rejected. They tried to decide which **candidate** the **citizen** had intended to vote for. To prevent cheating, **Democratic** and **Republican** officials observed the election workers.

RED - page 23 BLUE - page 47

A hearing before the Florida Supreme Court

Racing the Clock

Volusia and Broward **Counties** had hand recounted all of their **ballots** by 5 P.M. on November 26. But Palm Beach County missed the deadline by two hours. And Dade County had called off its recount because it could not meet the deadline.

Harris **certified** Florida's official **vote** total on November 26. The certification included all of the hand-recounted votes from Volusia and Broward Counties. It also included the **absentee ballot** votes. The certification made Bush Florida's winner. He won by 537 votes.

Harris's certification angered Gore. So the next day, he filed a **lawsuit** in a Florida **circuit court**. He wanted the court to overturn the certified **election** results. He wanted Palm Beach County's hand-recounted votes to be included in the official vote total. And he wanted Dade County to have an opportunity to recount all of its ballots.

On November 28, Dade and Palm Beach Counties sent their ballots to the circuit court as evidence. On December 4, the circuit court ruled against Gore. It said the official vote total was legal. So Gore **appealed** to the Florida **Supreme Court**.

RED - page 23 BLUE - page 47

Florida Secretary of State Katherine Harris certifies Florida's votes.

The U.S. Supreme Court

On December 4, the **U.S. Supreme Court** ruled on Bush's November 22 **lawsuit**. Bush had asked the **justices** to stop the Florida recount. But the justices did not stop it. Instead they sent the case back to the Florida Supreme Court.

The U.S. Supreme Court wanted the Florida Supreme Court to explain its decision to recount the **ballots** by hand. The U.S. Supreme Court feared that the Florida Supreme Court was creating new **election laws**. Making new laws is the **state legislature's** job. The courts can only interpret the laws.

The Florida Supreme Court responded two weeks later. They decided there was too little time to create a fair way to hand count all of the ballots.

Meanwhile, time was running out. Gore and Bush still had lawsuits in several different courts. Lawmakers worried Florida's 25 **electoral votes** would not be counted if the winner was not announced by December 12. That was the legal deadline for state legislatures to choose **electors**.

So on December 6, the Florida legislature called a **special session**. There, they decided what to do with Florida's electoral votes. Bush had already been **certified** the winner. So by law, Florida planned to give its 25 electoral votes to Bush if the lawsuits were not settled in time.

The Florida Supreme Court heard Gore's **appeal** on December 7. He wanted the court to overturn the official vote total. The next day, the court ruled in Gore's favor.

RED - page 23 BLUE - page 47

The **court** ordered a statewide hand recount of all the **ballots** that the counting machines had rejected on November 8. It also added 383 **votes** to Gore's total. Harris had refused to include these votes because they were late. Gore's chances for victory were growing.

Republicans and Democrats protest outside the U.S. Supreme Court Building.

ELECTION 200

Decision

On December 9, Bush filed two **lawsuits** to stop the statewide hand recounts. He filed one with the **U.S. Circuit Court of Appeals** in Atlanta. He filed the other with the **U.S. Supreme Court**.

Later that day, the U.S. Supreme Court stopped the statewide hand recounts. Then it agreed to hear Bush's **appeal**. On December 11, the court listened to **lawyers** representing Gore and Bush.

Gore's lawyers argued that the statewide hand recount was legal. They talked about the Tenth **Amendment**. It gives **states** control over their **election** processes. So they felt the **federal government** should not get involved.

Bush's lawyers argued that the statewide hand recount was illegal. They said the recounts were against the Fourteenth Amendment. They also said that Florida's Supreme Court had illegally made new **laws** by changing the deadline for **votes** to be counted.

On December 12, the **justices** ruled on the case. They called the Florida Supreme Court's decision **unconstitutional**. The U.S. Supreme Court said that according to the Fourteenth Amendment, the law equally protects each **citizen**. There were no rules in place for the hand recounts. So citizens' votes were being treated unequally.

The justices also stopped the statewide recount. They said it could not be finished by December 12. That was the day states had to choose their **electors**.

RED - page 23 BLUE - page 47

The ruling disappointed Gore and his **lawyers**. They looked for ways to continue fighting. But they found none. So on December 13, Gore **conceded** to Bush.

On December 18, **electors** from all 50 states met. They cast their **votes** for **president**. **Federal** and state **election** officials had received the electors' **certified** votes on December 27.

The **U.S. Congress** counted the **electoral votes** on January 2, 2001. Bush had 271 electoral votes. Gore had 267. George W. Bush became the forty-third president of the United States.

Vice President Al Gore congratulates President-elect George W. Bush.

Election 2000

November

7

Americans vote on election day. The election is too close to call in Florida.

8

Gore calls Bush to concede, then changes his mind. The Florida election is still too close to call.

9

Gore asks for a hand recount in four Florida counties.

11

Bush files a lawsuit in a U.S. District Court to stop hand recounts.

16

Bush asks the U.S. Circuit Court of Appeals to stop the recount. Gore files a lawsuit in a Florida circuit court to stop the certification of Florida's votes. The Florida court says no.

17

U.S. Circuit Court of Appeals rules against Bush. Gore appeals to the Florida Supreme Court. The court stops Harris from certifying Florida's votes.

21

The Florida Supreme Court orders the recount to continue.

22

Bush files a lawsuit with the U.S. Supreme Court to stop the recount.

6

The Florida legislature calls a special session to decide what to do with the state's electoral votes.

8

The Florida Supreme Court rules in Gore's favor. It orders a statewide recount.

9

Bush files lawsuits with the U.S. Supreme Court and the U.S. Circuit Court of Appeals. The U.S. Supreme Court stops Florida's statewide hand recount.

Timeline

13

U.S. District Court refuses to stop the recount. Two Florida counties file a lawsuit in a Florida circuit court to get more time to finish.

14

The Florida circuit court refuses to give the counties more time.

15

Bush asks a Florida circuit court to stop the recount. The court says no.

26

Harris certifies Florida's votes.

27

Gore files a lawsuit in a Florida circuit court to overturn the certified vote.

December

4

The U.S. Supreme Court sends Bush's case back to the Florida Supreme Court. The Florida circuit court rules against Gore. He appeals to the Florida Supreme Court.

12

The U.S. Supreme Court rules against Gore.

13

Gore concedes the election to Bush.

January 2001

20

Bush is sworn in as the forty-third U.S. president.

Part II

A Lesson in Civics

George W. Bush and Al Gore fought one of the most contested **presidential elections** in modern times. By the time Gore **conceded**, the whole world had learned a lesson about civics and American **democracy**.

America's **legislative** and **judicial** systems were pushed to the limit. For the first time, the **U.S. Supreme Court** helped decide who would be president.

Despite the heated election, there was a peaceful transfer of power. Troops did not need to bring about order. No tanks rolled down the streets of Washington, D.C. America's **Constitution** had passed a tough test.

So, what civics lessons did Election 2000 teach the world? The following pages explain the civics terms highlighted in **red** in Part I.

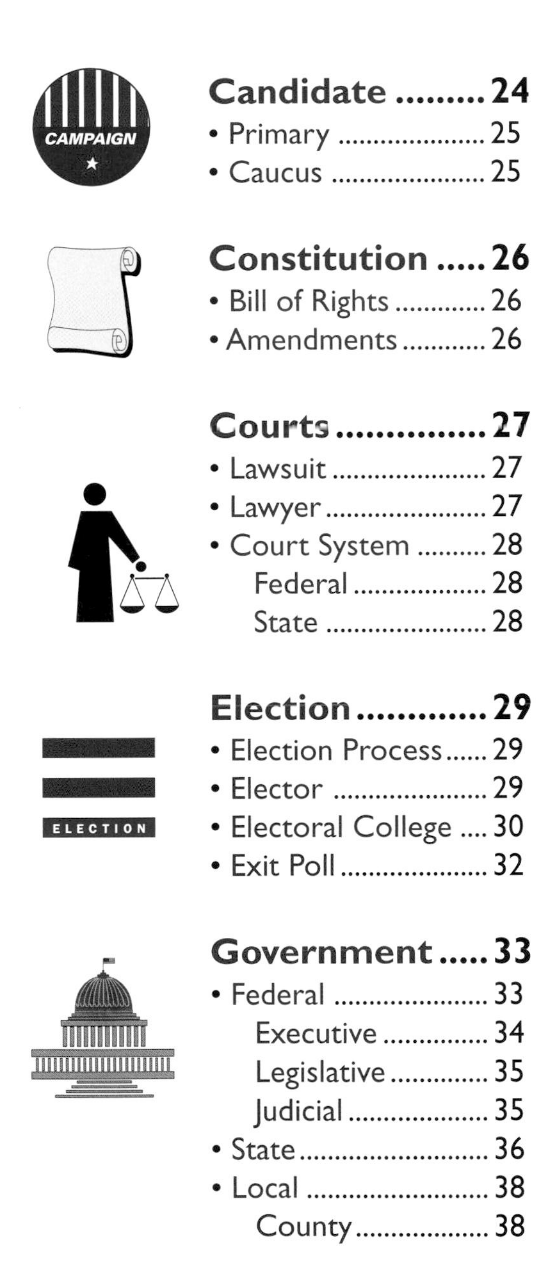

Candidate 24
- Primary 25
- Caucus 25

Constitution 26
- Bill of Rights 26
- Amendments 26

Courts 27
- Lawsuit 27
- Lawyer 27
- Court System 28
    - Federal 28
    - State 28

Election 29
- Election Process 29
- Elector 29
- Electoral College 30
- Exit Poll 32

Government 33
- Federal 33
    - Executive 34
    - Legislative 35
    - Judicial 35
- State 36
- Local 38
    - County 38

Laws 40
- Lawmaking Process 40

Political Parties 42
- Democrats 42
- Republicans 42

President 42
- Republic 42
- Democracy 42
- President's Jobs 43

Voting 44
- Voting Process 44
- Citizen 45
- Ballot 46
- Polling Place 46
- Popular Vote 46

Candidate

What is a candidate?

A candidate is a person who runs for political office.

How is a candidate chosen?

In every presidential election, many candidates run for president. Some belong to the same political party. But each party can have only one candidate in the presidential election.

1

The political parties hold primaries or caucuses in each state.

2

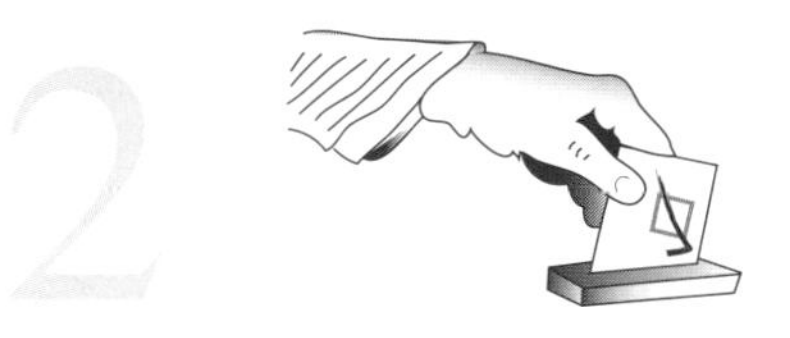

Each primary and caucus chooses a candidate. Often, many different candidates are chosen.

3

The chosen candidates travel throughout the country. They make public appearances and give speeches.

4

Each party holds a national convention. There, each party chooses one candidate from the primary and caucus winners to represent it in the presidential election.

What is a primary?

A primary is an election. In most primaries, political party members of a state vote for candidates from their party. In some primaries, citizens don't have to be party members to vote.

What is a caucus?

A caucus is a meeting of political party leaders. In a caucus, party leaders of a state choose a candidate from their party.

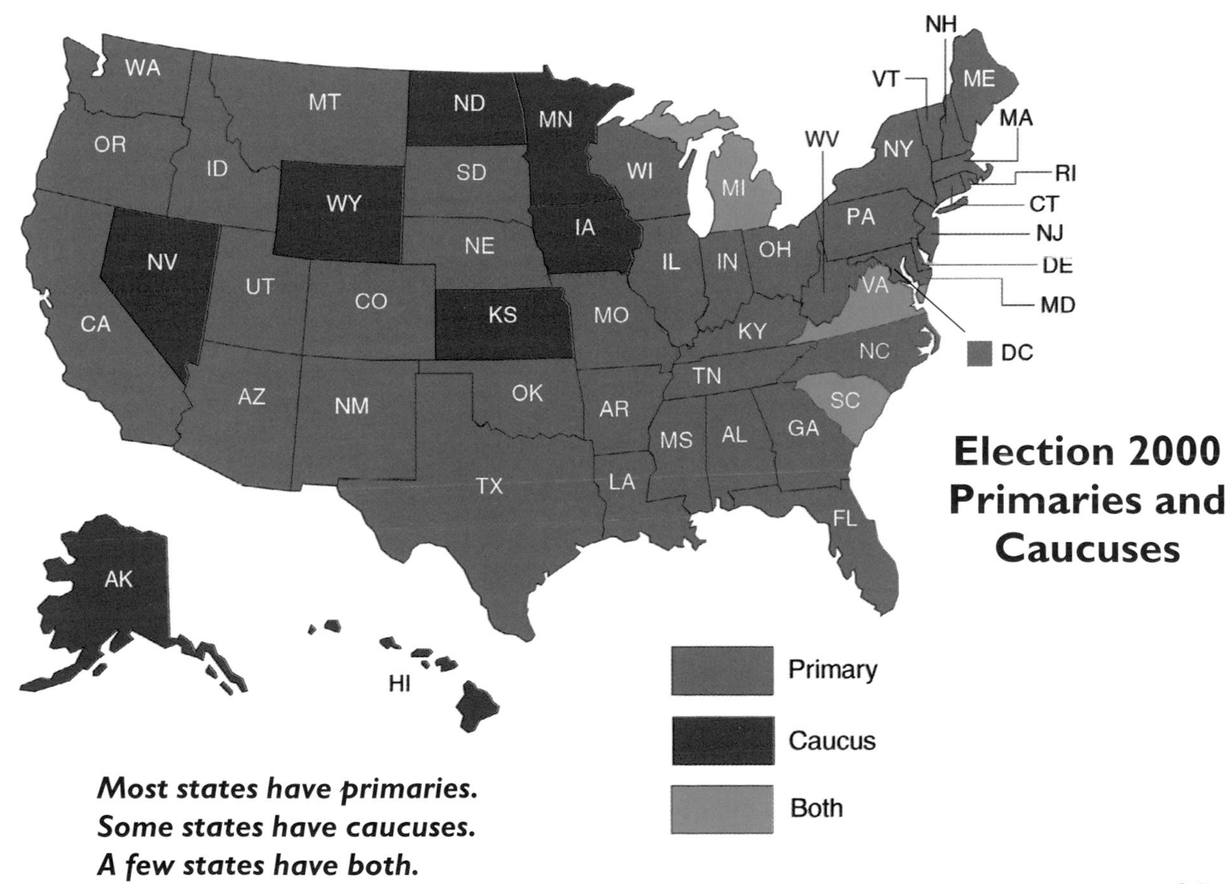

Most states have primaries. Some states have caucuses. A few states have both.

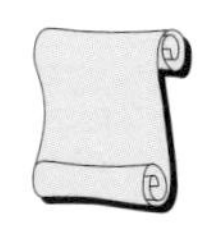

Constitution

What is a constitution?

A constitution is a written plan for government. It says how a country's or state's government will be organized. America and all its states have constitutions.

The U.S. Constitution

What is the U.S. Constitution?

The U.S. Constitution describes the structure of the federal government and the rights of the American people. The U.S. Constitution also includes the Bill of Rights.

What is the Bill of Rights?

The Bill of Rights is the first ten amendments to the U.S. Constitution. It gives citizens certain freedoms and rights, including the right to vote.

What is an amendment?

An amendment is a change to the Constitution. A member of Congress proposes the amendment. Two-thirds of each house of Congress must approve a proposed amendment, and three-fourths of the states must **ratify** it.

Court

What is a court?

A court is a place were legal cases are decided or where trials are held.

What do courts do?

Courts use the law to settle disagreements between people, between people and the government, and between governments.

Courts decide in favor of one side or another. The losing side can ask for a new trial from a higher court. This is called an **appeal**.

A court decision can be appealed all the way to the U.S. Supreme Court. It is the highest court in America. Once the Supreme Court makes a decision, it is final. No more appeals can be made.

How does the court system work?

Overall, there are 51 court systems in the U.S. There is one system for each state and one for the federal government. Federal courts work together with state courts. Federal courts deal with cases involving constitutional law. State courts deal with cases involving their own constitution.

What is a lawsuit?

A lawsuit is a case in a court of law. Lawsuits are started by one person to claim something from another. Lawsuits are filed in courts, often by lawyers.

What is a lawyer?

A lawyer is a person who knows the law. A lawyer gives advice about matters of law or acts for others in a court of law.

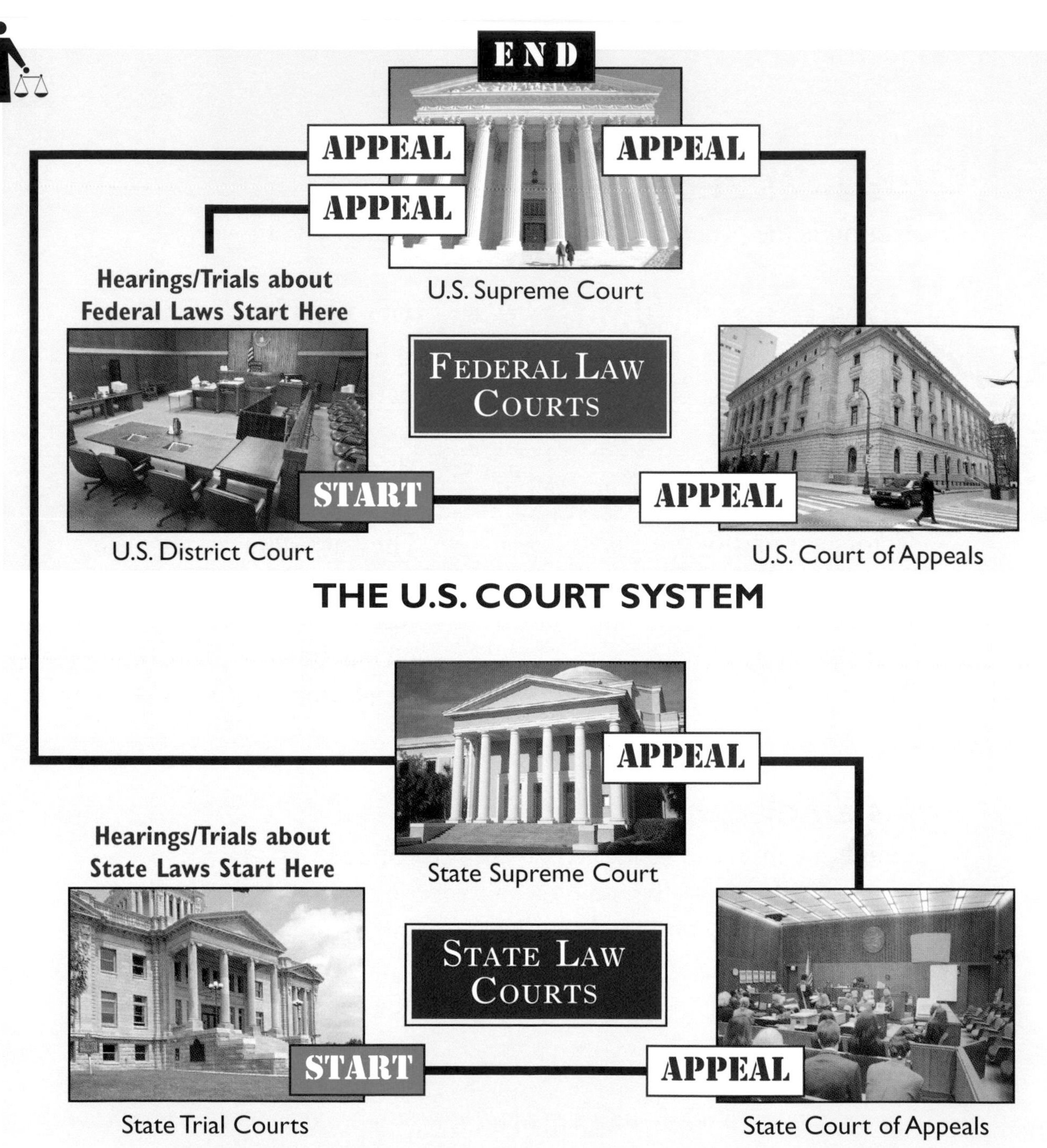

In Maryland and New York, the highest court is the state court of appeals.

Election

What is an election?

An election is the process of choosing a candidate by voting.

How does the presidential election work?

The U.S. Constitution states that a presidential election is to be held every four years. It must be held on the Tuesday after the first Monday in November.

In a presidential election, people do not vote directly for a presidential candidate. Instead, they vote for a group of people known as electors. These electors are part of the electoral college. They are supposed to vote for the candidate who wins the state's popular vote. By winning a state, the candidate receives all the state's electoral votes.

When the election is over, Congress totals each candidate's electoral votes. The candidate who receives the majority of electoral votes wins the presidency.

What is an elector?

An elector is a member of the U.S. electoral college. The U.S. Constitution says that state legislatures can choose their electors. Their number must equal the number of the state's members in Congress.

Candidates for elector are often chosen at party conventions, in primary elections, or by party organizations. Officers of the federal government cannot be electors.

How does the electoral college work?

The electoral college is the system used to elect the president and vice president. The **Founding Fathers** created it so that both Congress and citizens have a role in the presidential election.

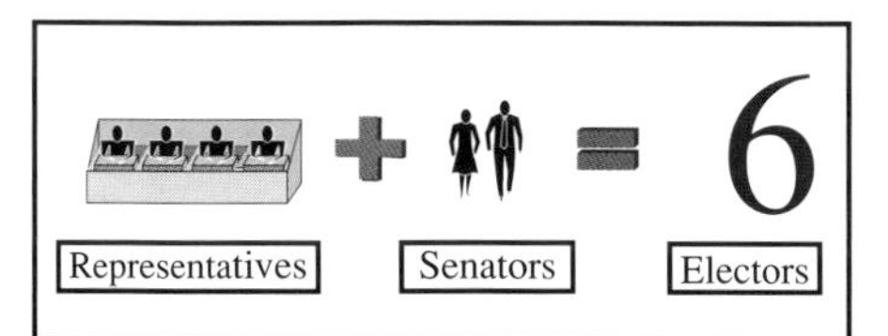

1 **Political parties in each state appoint electors. Each state gets one elector for each senator and representative it has in Congress. Each elector has one electoral vote.**

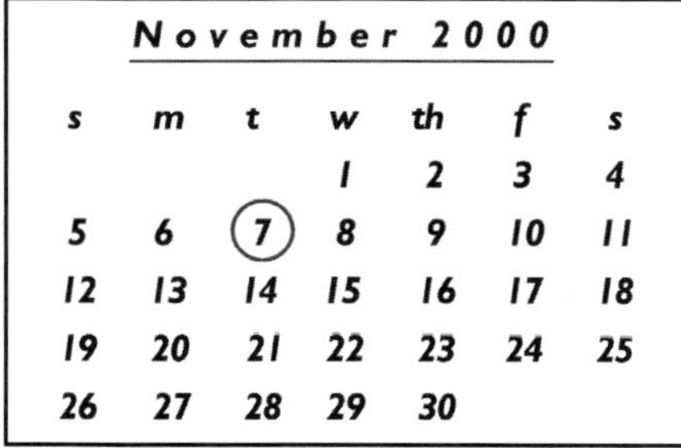

November 2000

s	m	t	w	th	f	s
			1	2	3	4
5	6	7	8	9	10	11
12	13	14	15	16	17	18
19	20	21	22	23	24	25
26	27	28	29	30		

2 **On the Tuesday after the first Monday in November, the citizens of each state cast a popular vote for president.**

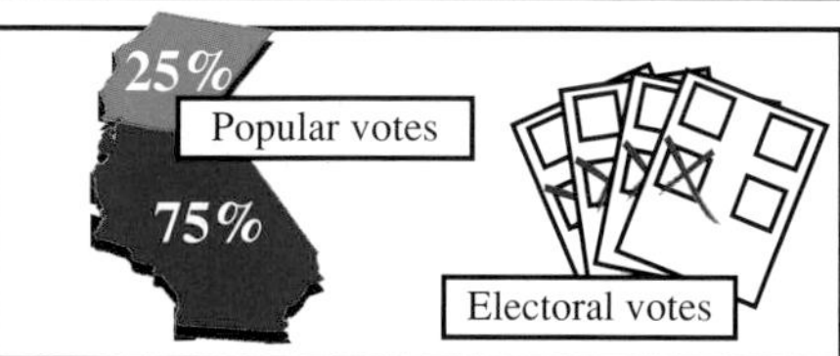

3 **The candidate who wins a state's popular vote gets all the state's electoral votes.**

December 2000

s	m	t	w	th	f	s
					1	2
3	4	5	6	7	8	9
10	11	12	13	14	15	16
17	18	19	20	21	22	23
24	25	26	27	28	29	30
31						

4 **On the Monday after the second Wednesday in December, each state's electors cast their votes for their state's winning candidate. Then they send the votes to Congress.**

January 2001

s	m	t	w	th	f	s
	1	2	3	4	5	(6)
7	8	9	10	11	12	13
14	15	16	17	18	19	20
21	22	23	24	25	26	27
28	29	30	31			

5

On the sixth day of January the following year, Congress counts the states' electoral votes. The president of the Senate announces the winner.

6

The new president is inaugurated on January 20.

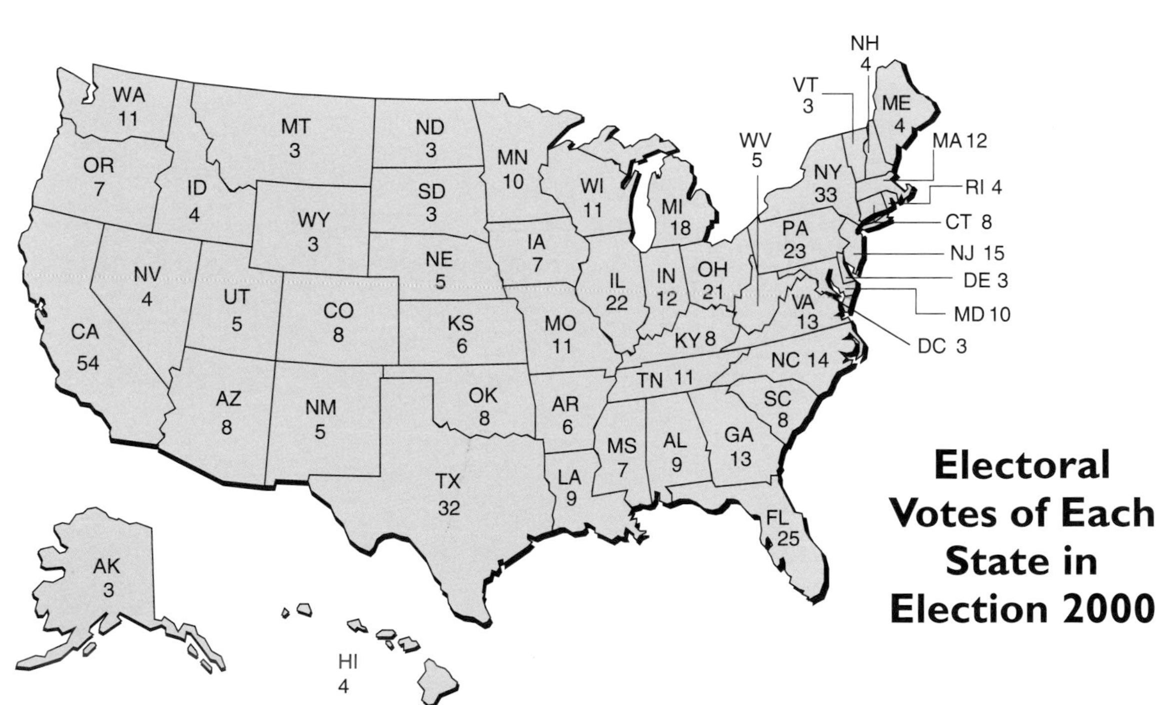

Electoral Votes of Each State in Election 2000

What is an exit poll?

An exit poll is a survey. It takes place as voters exit their polling place. People called pollsters conduct exit polls. They ask people who they voted for and why.

Pollsters do not ask every voter to take the exit poll. This would take too long. Instead, pollsters pick just a few voters out of many. These voters help the pollsters guess how all the people at the polling place voted.

Exit polls have two important jobs. First, they allow the pollsters to announce the winner before the votes are counted. Second, they explain why people voted as they did.

How does an exit poll work?

1

The pollster asks some voters to take an exit poll.

2

The pollster gives the voters a form to fill out. It asks them who they voted for and why.

3

The pollster collects the forms. She adds up which candidate won more votes in the exit poll.

4

The pollster calls the television stations. She tells the stations which candidate won the exit poll.

5

The stations use the exit poll to guess the winner.

Government

What is a government?

A government is a group of people who use laws to run a country, state, county, district, city, or town. In the United States, there are federal, state, and local governments.

What is the federal government?

The federal government is the main government of the United States. It was formed to help the country run better and protect its citizens.

The U.S. Constitution divides the federal government into three branches. They are the executive, legislative, and judicial branches.

Federal Government

Make treaties

Have an army and navy

Run post offices

Declare war

Oversee business between states and other countries

Decide how to treat other countries

Print money

TREATY

Letters

These are the things ONLY the federal government can do.

What is the executive branch of the federal government?

The executive branch makes sure people follow the laws that the legislative branch makes. The leaders of this branch are the president and vice president. The president lives at the White House in Washington, D.C.

The president chooses cabinet members and department heads. But the **Senate** must approve his or her choices.

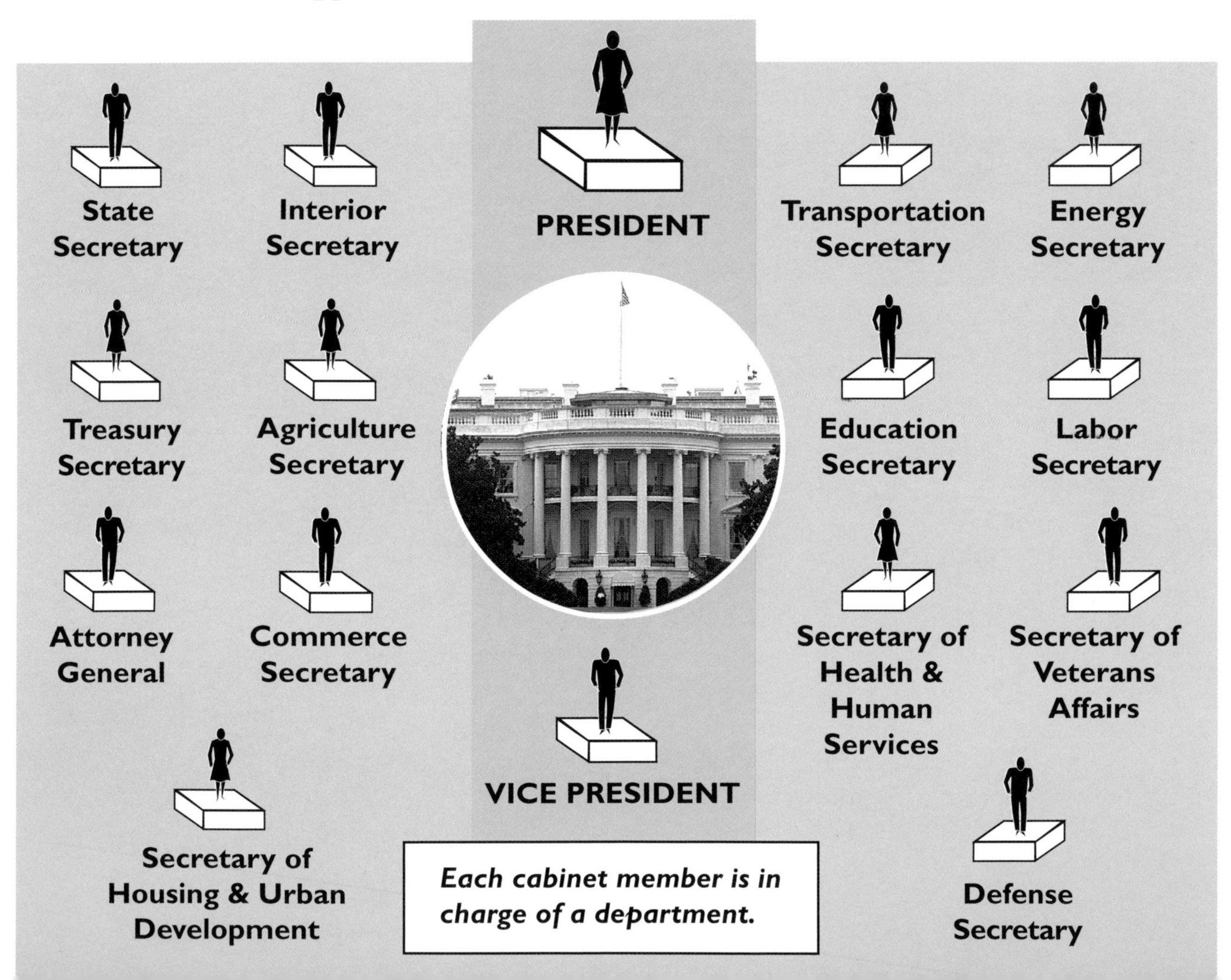

Each cabinet member is in charge of a department.

What is the legislative branch of the federal government?

The legislative branch makes laws for the country. Its main group is known as Congress. Congress is made up of two parts, the **House of Representatives** and the **Senate**. Congress meets at the U.S. Capitol in Washington, D.C.

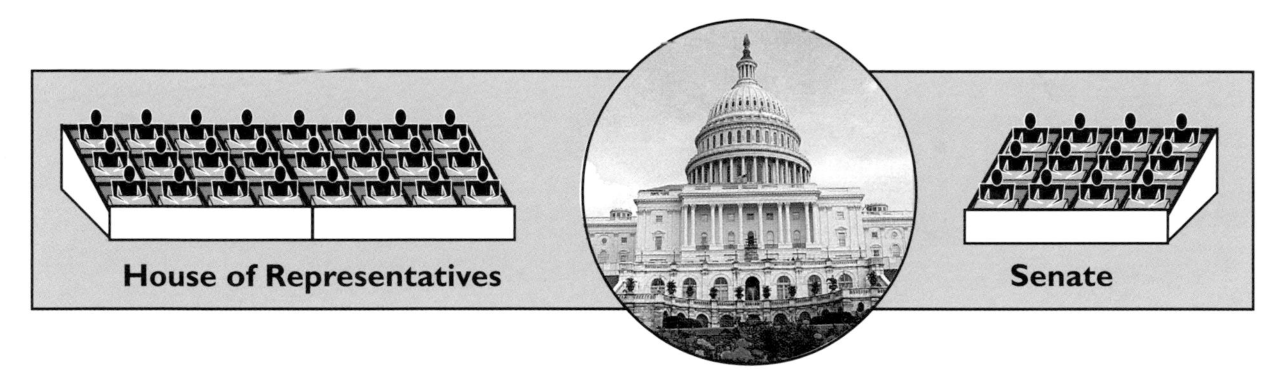

The U.S. Congress has two parts.

What is the judicial branch of the federal government?

The judicial branch makes decisions about the meaning of laws. The judicial branch is made up of courts. The highest of these courts is the U.S. Supreme Court. The Supreme Court is made up of nine **justices**. They meet at the Supreme Court Building in Washington, D.C.

What is a state government?

A state government is a group of people, organizations, and laws in charge of a state. State governments have all powers not given to the federal government by the U.S. Constitution.

Each state uses its own constitution as the basis for its laws. All state constitutions are different. That's because each state has its own history, needs, beliefs, and geography.

Each state's constitution is similar to the U.S. Constitution. All state constitutions must obey the laws in the U.S. Constitution.

Each state's constitution separates power into three branches: executive, legislative, and judicial. In all states except one, the legislative branch has a senate and a house of representatives. In Nebraska, the state legislature only has one house.

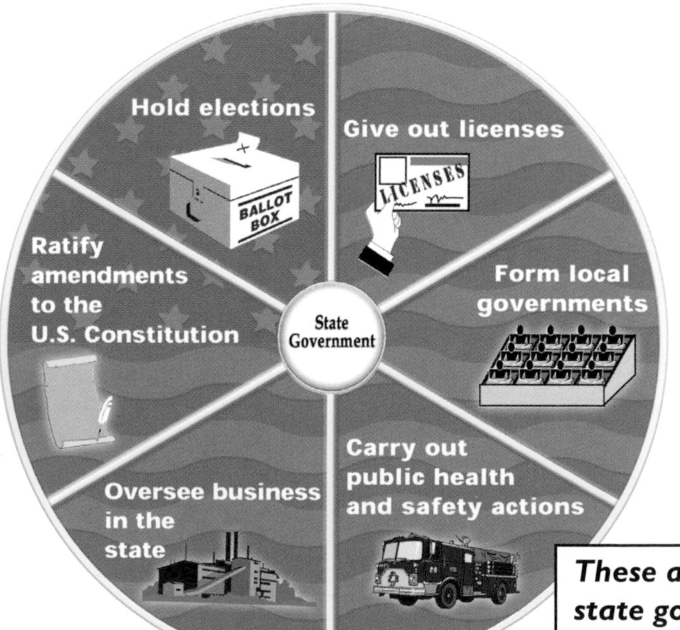

These are the things ONLY the state government can do.

CONSTITUTION		
EXECUTIVE	**LEGISLATIVE**	**JUDICIAL**
• Propose plans and policies • Make day-to-day decisions • Administer and enforce laws	• Make laws • Set long-term policies • Respond to individual and group concerns	• Interpret existing laws and policies • Apply laws to individual cases

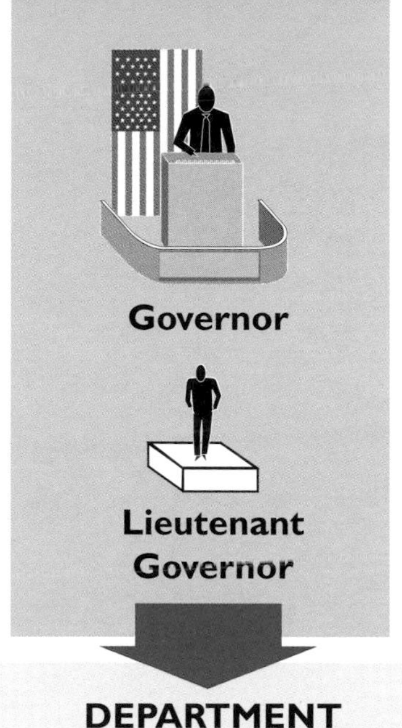

The Executive Branch of State Government

DEPARTMENT HEADS

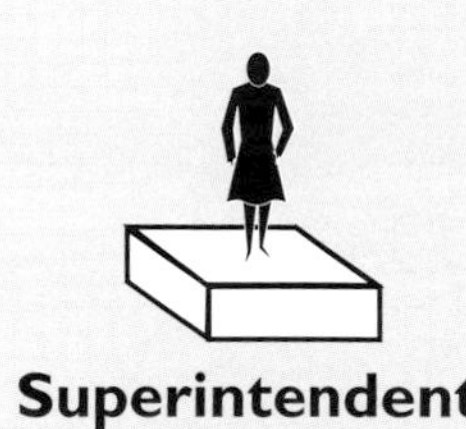

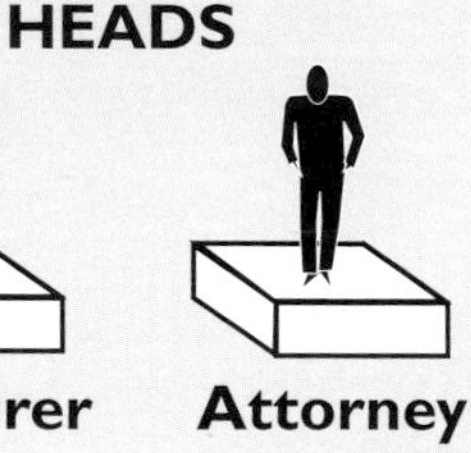

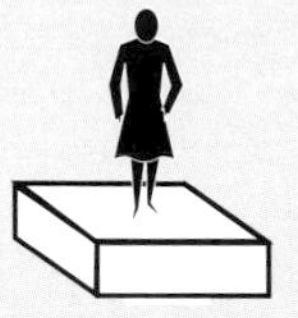

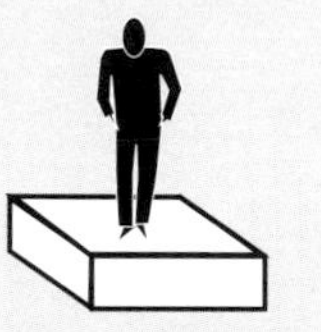

Why does America have states?

America was once made up of thirteen colonies. They were ruled by England. In 1776, the colonies declared their independence. After the colonies won the Revolutionary War, they became states. Each state formed its own government.

A federal government was created when the states **ratified** the U.S. Constitution in 1787. It divided power between the federal and state governments. And it helped unite America. But it also allowed the states to govern themselves.

What is a local government?

A local government is a group of people, organizations, and laws in charge of a county, city, town, or district. Local governments get their powers from their state's constitution.

Most Americans live under several local governments. There are five forms of local government:

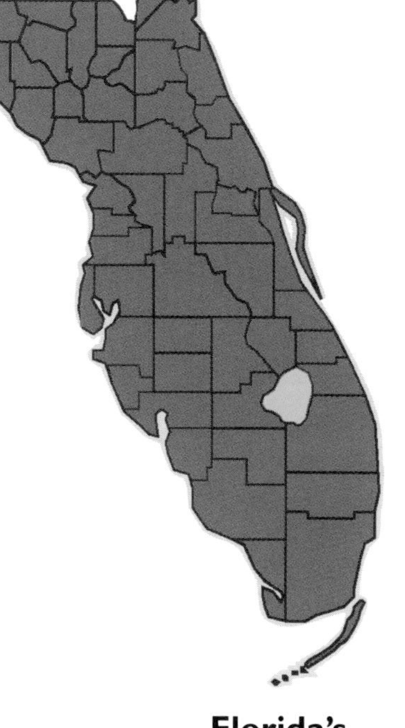

Florida's Counties

1. **County** - often the largest unit of local government. Most states, except Connecticut and Rhode Island, are divided into counties.
2. **Township** - a smaller unit of a county. Townships are the least common form of local government in America.
3. **Municipality** - areas that are **incorporated** and often include cities.
4. **Special District** - the most common local government in America. They are formed to meet special needs of an area, like farmland.
5. **School District** - an area that provides local schools. A board of education oversees a school district.

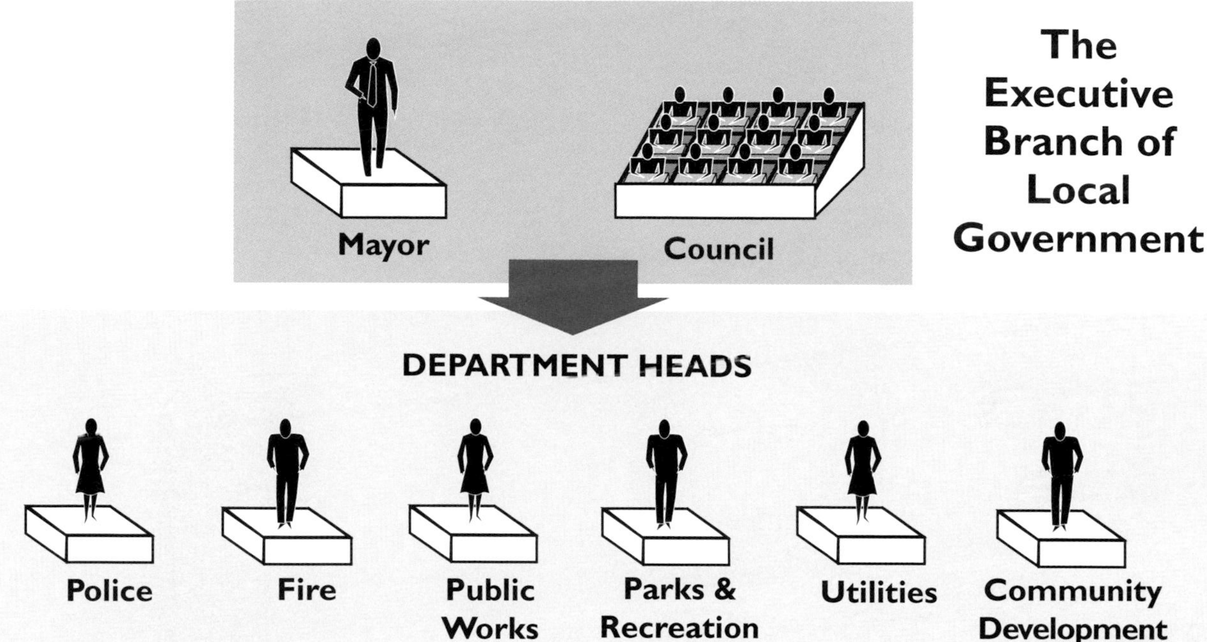

Most local governments in America follow the mayor-council form.

What is a precinct?

A precinct is a part of a county, city, town, or district. But it does not have its own government. Precincts are formed to help organize an area for voting and police protection.

Laws

What is a law?

A law is a rule made by a country or state to protect its citizens.

Who makes laws?

Congress makes laws. A law begins as a bill. A bill is a written idea for a new law. Bills can be introduced in the **House of Representatives** or the **Senate**. When a bill is approved, it becomes a law.

If a bill begins in the House, representatives vote on it first. If it passes, the bill goes to the Senate for approval. If a bill begins in the Senate, senators vote on it first. If it passes, the bill goes to the House for approval.

A bill can die at any point in this process. A bill dies when not enough people vote in favor of it. A bill can die in a committee, in the House, or in the Senate.

1 How a Bill Becomes a Law

- **A representative introduces a bill to the House.**

- **The House sends the bill to a committee. It reviews the bill. Sometimes, the committee makes changes to the bill.**

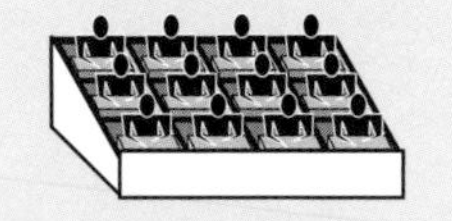

- **The committee sends the bill back to the House. Representatives debate the bill. Then they vote on it.**

2

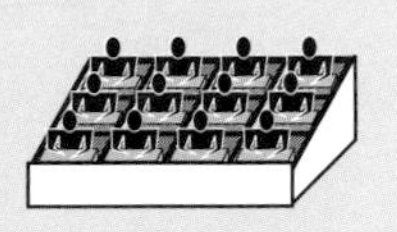

- The House sends the approved bill to the Senate.

- The Senate sends the bill to a committee. It reviews the bill. It can make changes to the bill.

- The committee sends the bill back to the Senate. Senators debate the bill. Then they vote on it.

- The approved bill goes to a committee of House and Senate members. They meet to agree on final changes to the bill.

3

Congress sends the bill to the president, who studies it.

THE BILL BECOMES A LAW IF:

- The president signs it.
- The president does not sign it for ten days while Congress is in session.

- If two-thirds of Congress vote in favor of the bill, it becomes a law.

THE BILL DOES NOT BECOME A LAW IF:

- The president vetoes it.

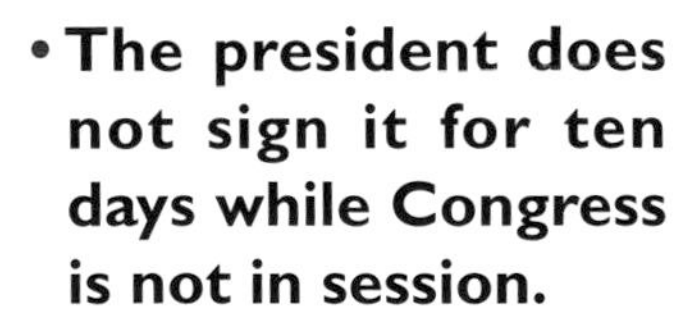

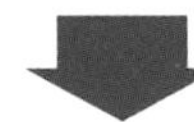

- The bill goes back to Congress. The Senate and the House vote on the bill again.

- The president does not sign it for ten days while Congress is not in session.

Political Parties

What is a political party?

A political party is a group of people with similar political ideas. They try to put their ideas into action by electing a party member to the government.

Anyone can form a political party. But not all parties are included on a state's presidential ballot. To get its candidate's name on a ballot, a party must often have thousands of members.

What are the main political parties in America?

There are many political parties in America. But the Republican and Democratic parties have been the main parties since the 1860s.

Most Americans call themselves Republicans or Democrats. Republicans favor a small government. Democrats favor a large government.

Every president since 1856 has been either a Republican or a Democrat. Since World War II ended, Republican and Democratic candidates have received almost all of the votes in the presidential elections.

President

What is a president?

The president is the highest official of a modern republic.

What is a republic?

A republic is a government that has a chief of state who is not a monarch and who is usually a president.

What is a democracy?

A democracy is a government run by the people who live under it.

The 7 "Hats" of the U.S. President

A president is elected or re-elected every four years.

A president can serve only two terms. Each term lasts four years.

To be president, a person:

- must have lived in the country for at least 14 years.
- must be a U.S. citizen born in America.
- must be at least 35 years old.

If a president dies in office, the vice president becomes president.

Chief of State

- Performs official duties
- Stands as a symbol of the United States

Chief Diplomat

- Oversees relations with other countries
- Writes treaties
- Grants recognition to new governments

Chief Legislator

- Proposes laws
- Reports to Congress

Chief Jurist

- Appoints federal judges
- Enforces court ruling

Chief Politician

- Leads political party
- Supports its candidates

Commander-in-Chief

- Constructs military plans
- Maintains control of armed forces

Chief Executive

- Oversees government programs
- Manages government workers

Voting

What is a vote?

A vote is a way for a citizen to choose a candidate for office.

How does the voting process work?

1. The voter goes to the polling place in his or her precinct to vote.

2. Election workers give the voter a paper ballot.

3. The voter goes to a voting booth and marks his or her choice on the ballot.

4. The voter places his or her ballot in a ballot box.

5. Election workers count all the ballots by machine or by hand.

6. Election officials make sure the voting results are right. They send them to their secretary of state.

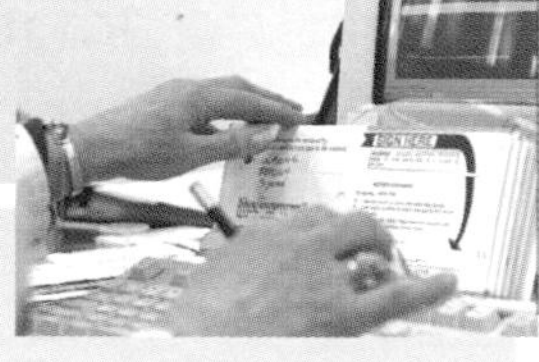

7. The secretary of state declares which candidate will receive the state's electoral votes.

8. Federal election officials receive the voting results.

9. State electors meet to cast their votes for president.

10. The president of the U.S. Senate reads the election results to Congress. Whoever receives the majority of the electoral votes wins the presidential election.

Who can vote?

Vote

American citizens 18 years old or older can vote in national, state, and local elections.

Each state decides the rules for voting in elections. But all states must follow the U.S. Constitution's rules about voting. The U.S. Constitution says that states cannot deny a citizen's right to vote based on race, color, or sex.

The right to vote is one of an American citizen's most important rights. By voting, citizens directly affect the actions of their government.

American citizens using voting machines to vote

Who is an American citizen?

- A person born in the U.S.

- A person born to U.S. citizens living or traveling in foreign countries.

- A person born in a foreign country who has become a naturalized citizen.

Who is a naturalized citizen?

A naturalized citizen is someone from another country who becomes an American citizen. A person becomes a naturalized citizen by filling out an application and passing a citizenship test.

What is a ballot?

A ballot is a device used to cast a vote. A vote may be cast by paper ballot, by voting machine, by computer punch card, or by computer.

Citizens who are ill, physically disabled, or away from home can use an **absentee ballot** to vote. An absentee ballot is obtained from a local, county, or city election office.

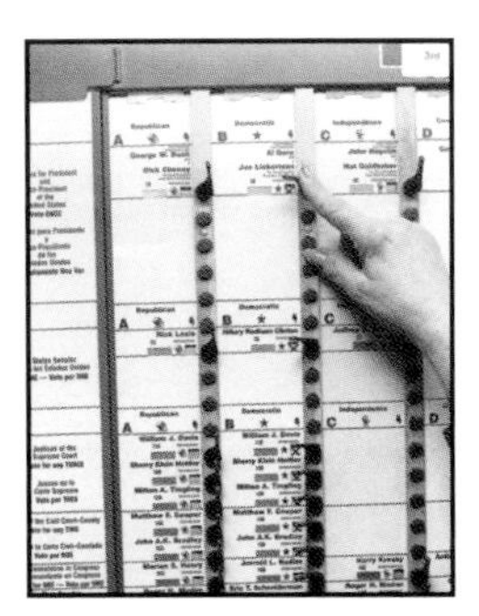

A mechanical voting machine

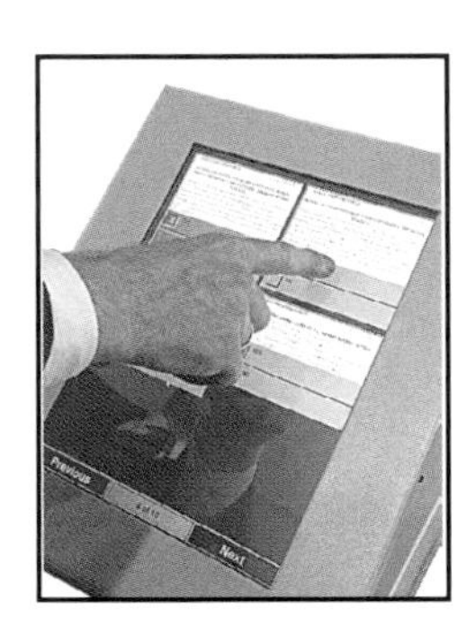

An electronic voting machine

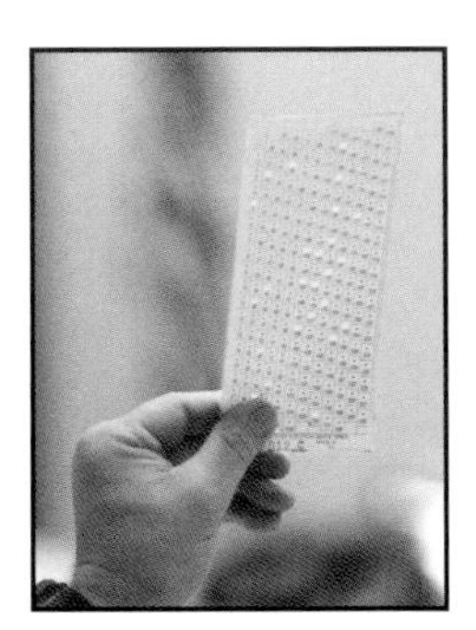

A computer punch card

What is a polling place?

A polling place is where people go to vote. Public buildings like schools or community centers are often used as polling places.

What is the popular vote?

The popular vote is the total vote from all the states. It is made by citizens who are registered to vote.

Glossary

absentee ballot - a ballot mailed to a polling place before an election. Voters who cannot travel to their polling places on election day use absentee ballots.
accurate - free of errors.
appeal - to ask a high court to review the decision of a low court.
campaign - to give speeches and tell people your ideas so they will vote you into an elected office.
certify - to make official.
commission - a group of people appointed or elected to do certain things.
concede - to admit something. Candidates concede defeat in elections after they realize they have lost.
debate - to discuss a question or topic, often publicly.
Founding Fathers - the men who attended the Constitutional Convention in Philadelphia in 1787. They helped write the U.S. Constitution.
hearing - the opportunity to present one's case in a court of law.
House of Representatives - the lower House in the U.S. Congress. Citizens elect members of the House to make laws for the nation.
incorporated - formed into a legal corporation, which gives a city or town certain rights and privileges.
justice - a judge for the U.S. Supreme Court.
nominate - to name as a candidate for an office.
ratify - to officially approve.
secretary of state - a state official who keeps official records and the state seal. He or she also oversees elections, issues drivers licenses, and serves as the state librarian.
Senate - the upper house of the U.S. Congress. The senate has two members from each state of the Union.
special session - the U.S. Congress usually meets every year beginning in January and extending until its business is concluded. If Congress meets again after the session ends for the year, this meeting is called a special session.
unconstitutional - something that goes against the laws of the U.S. Constitution.

For Further Reading

Gutman, Dan. *Landslide! A Kid's Guide to the U.S. Elections*. New York: Aladdin Paperbacks, 2000.

Maestro, Betsy. *A More Perfect Union: The Story of Our Constitution*. New York: Lothrop, Lee and Shepard Books, 1987.

Sobel, Syl. *How the U.S. Government Works*. Hauppauge, NY: Barron's Juveniles, 1999.

Internet Sites

- **Ben's Guide to U.S. Government for Kids** http://bensguide.gpo.gov/
  Benjamin Franklin teaches kids from kindergarten through twelfth grade all about the federal government.
- **Kids Voting USA** http://www.kidsvotingusa.org/
  A nonprofit organization dedicated to securing democracy for the future by involving youth in the election process today.
- **PBS Kids Democracy Project** http://www.pbs.org/democracy/kids/
  Find out how government works, step inside a voting booth, and find out what could happen if you were president for a day.

These sites are subject to change. For more sites, go to your favorite search engine and enter "election," "government," or "voting."

Index

B
Bush, George W. 4, 6, 8, 10, 11, 12, 14, 16, 18, 19, 22

C
citizenship 45
Clinton, Bill 7
Congress, U.S. 4, 19, 26, 29, 30, 31, 35, 40, 41, 44
  House of Representatives 6, 7, 35, 40, 41
  Senate 7, 31, 34, 35, 40, 41, 44
constitution, state 26, 36, 38
Constitution, U.S. 10, 11, 18, 22, 26, 29, 33, 36, 37, 45
  amendments 10, 11, 18, 26
  Bill of Rights 26

D
democracy 22, 42
Democratic party 4, 6, 7, 12, 22,

E
election (presidential) 29, 32, 42, 44
  candidate 6, 12, 24, 25, 29, 30, 42, 44
  caucus 24, 25
  national convention 24
  primary 24, 25
Election of 1876 4
electoral college 29, 30
electoral votes 4, 8, 16, 19, 29, 30, 31, 44
electors 16, 18, 19, 29, 30, 44
exit poll 8, 32

F
federal court
  U.S. Circuit Court of Appeals 11, 18, 28
  U.S. District Court 10, 28
  U.S. Supreme Court 4, 12, 16, 18, 22, 27, 28, 35
federal government 10, 11, 18, 19, 29, 33, 36, 37
  executive branch 33, 34
  judicial branch 22, 27, 28, 33, 35
  legislative branch 22, 33, 34, 35
Florida
  certified vote total 11, 12, 14
  circuit court 11, 14
  hand recount 10, 11, 12, 14, 16, 17, 18
  machine recount 8, 10
  Supreme Court 12, 14, 16, 17, 18
Founding Fathers 30

G
Gore, Al 4, 6, 7, 8, 10, 11, 12, 14, 16, 17, 18, 19, 22

H
Harris, Katherine 10, 11, 12, 14, 17
Hayes, Rutherford B. 4

L
law
  approval process 40, 41
  lawsuit 10, 11, 12, 14, 16, 18, 27
  lawyer 10, 18, 19, 27
local government 33, 38, 39

P
political parties 24, 30, 42
president 4, 6, 7, 19, 24, 29, 30, 31, 34, 41, 42, 43

R
republic 42
Republican party 4, 6, 12, 42

S
state court 27, 28
state government 10, 11, 18, 33, 36, 37, 38

T
Tilden, Samuel 4

V
vote
  ballot 8, 10, 11, 12, 14, 16, 17, 19, 42, 44, 46
  polling place 8, 44, 46
  popular vote 30, 44, 46
  voting process 30, 44